VIDEO BOOK

ARLEN ROTH TEACHES
FINGERSTYLE BLUES GUITAR

T0070718

Cover Photo by Tom Gage

To access video visit:
www.halleonard.com/mylibrary

Enter Code
2702-5917-0625-4980

ISBN 978-1-4950-6282-7

HAL•LEONARD®

7777 W. BLUEMOUND RD. P.O. BOX 13819 MILWAUKEE, WI 53213

In Australia Contact:
Hal Leonard Australia Pty. Ltd.
4 Lentara Court
Cheltenham, Victoria, 3192 Australia
Email: ausadmin@halleonard.com.au

Visit Hal Leonard Online at
www.halleonard.com

CONTENTS

Hello everyone and welcome to *Fingerstyle Blues Guitar*. This particular lesson deals with the basics of getting started in fingerstyle guitar—one of the most rewarding ways of playing the guitar on this planet! Much of this information I have learned and taught to others over the years. There is almost nothing more rewarding than sitting down and truly creating a fingerstyle piece that you can call your own, and that can make you feel like a "one man band!" This is how we can recreate and take even further the great stylings of folks such as Merle Travis, Chet Atkins, Mark Knopfler, Blind Blake, and many more.

About the Video

Each chapter in the book includes a full video lesson, so you can see and hear the material being taught. To access all of the videos that accompany this book, simply visit **www.halleonard.com/mylibrary** and enter the code found on page 1. The music examples that include video demonstrations are marked with an icon throughout the book, and the timecode listed with each icon tells you exactly where on the video the example is performed.

First thing's first… let's make sure we're in tune.

 Tuning notes

Now that we're in tune, let's get started!

CHAPTER 1:
BASIC TECHNIQUE

In this book, we are really working on the fundamentals of right-hand technique in fingerstyle playing. As you will see, the foundation I had from some classical guitar lessons at the very early age of 10 gave me a great respect for the right hand and its need to control the six strings. This includes the dedication of the fingers to certain strings as well as muting, dampening, arpeggio patterns, constant bass, and alternating bass.

Right-Hand Position (2:35)

Try getting used to the feel of the fingers on the strings with this simple exercise. After plucking the strings, dampen each one again with the same finger before plucking again. The fingers of the right hand are indicated as such throughout:

- *p* = thumb
- *i* = index
- *m* = middle
- *a* = ring

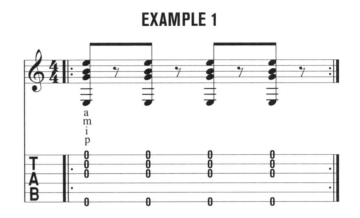

EXAMPLE 1

I see many students who get their picking hands all twisted up in positions that make no sense, but yet they try to carry on in those positions, even though they get held back by them! In the video, you'll see how important it is to dedicate those fingers to certain groups of strings and how, after a while, your fingers will develop a sense of knowing just where and when to place themselves. The coordination of the left and right hands is critical to good guitar playing, and the more you do it, the more they will become coordinated together!

Try a few variations now with an E chord using different finger groups in the right hand.

 (3:38)

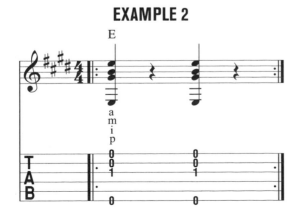

EXAMPLE 2

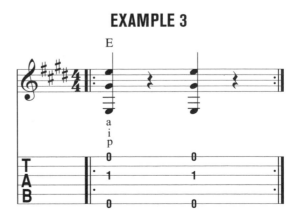

EXAMPLE 3

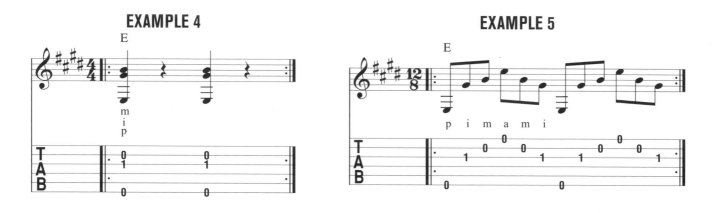

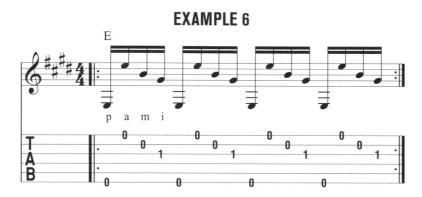

You can also see that the angle of my picking hand and how it strikes the strings is critical to good execution, as well as good tone. You do need to grow nails for this so that when you pick the strings they are sounded by both some nail and some skin. Obviously, if we only played with our nails, there would be no real sensation of actually touching the strings at all! So, the fingers come up slightly towards the palm after picking the strings, and most importantly, the thumb plays just ahead of the three-fingered group of index, middle, and ring. In this way, the thumb and index finger are never on a collision course, and they can feel free to create as much volume and/or subtlety as you want them to.

As you can see, the simple exercise of plucking the strings and then stopping them with the same finger(s) is a good way to get used to dedicating your fingers to certain strings. This also helps you feel the "shapes" of what you will be playing. When it comes to fingerpicking, it's really the *only* way we have to play strings simultaneously, save for using a pick and fingers together (hybrid picking).

If you notice, my thumb strikes the bass notes slightly on the side of the thumb, getting some nail and some skin. The action comes from the large thumb joint that's attached to the palm, as opposed to trying to pick it like the fingers do on their respective strings. It's different!

Accent Stroke

I'm also utilizing what is referred to as an *accent stroke* (or *rest stroke*) to play the bass notes, which simply means the thumb comes to rest on the next string. This approach helps us do two things: it keeps the thumb under control so it can't accidentally play an errant note or string, and it also serves to mute that next string, keeping it quiet. I always like to say that, often times, a note that is played also does something else to stop another note from being played. This occurs more often with the fretting hand, but in this case of the right hand, it also applies.

As you can see, using the thumb in the proper way always tells the thumb just how far it needs to "throw" to strike the bass note. Regardless of how loud or soft you want to play it, it never loses the position that's necessary.

Try playing what's called a *constant bass* figure with the thumb on the low E string in swung eighth notes, remembering to use the accent stroke.

(6:30)

EXAMPLE 7

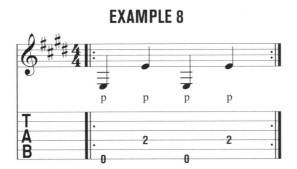

In the same way that it lands on the A string after striking the low E, the thumb can utilize this same accent stroke for muting as you play the alternating bass of, for example, a Travis picking piece. In this manner, it strikes the low E, lands on the A, strikes the D, and then lands on the G. If this is done correctly, even though we are plucking two strings, we are also stopping (or muting) two other strings! So now, with one movement of the thumb, we are literally controlling all four bottom strings!

 (7:28)

EXAMPLE 8

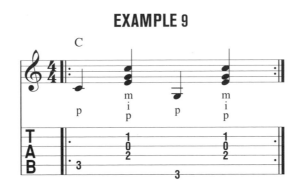

Most students seem to miss this important stylistic approach. It shows the real way to play the bass notes. Many players think that, to play an alternating bass pattern, they must hop over the string in the middle (if there is one)! Instead, and as you'll see in the video, the thumb lands quickly and then lands again. It may seem more complex than hopping over, but it is much more controlled and much more accurate than you may even know right now.

In chords with a root on the fifth string, such as a C chord, you can also alternate the bass in a pattern of string 5-string 4-string 6-string 4, like this:

 (10:52)

EXAMPLE 9

CHAPTER 2:
HARMONY SHUFFLES

As you will see, the "shuffle riff" positions will vary a bit depending on which chord forms we are working with. They're easiest to play when based off the open chord forms of E, A, or D, so we'll look at each.

E Chord Harmony Shuffle

You hear riffs involving two adjacent strings in the low end of the E, A, or D forms all the time. This means that we are only playing those two notes, which actually create what is often called the *power chord*. It's basically the root note and the 5th of the chord. The second moving note of the shuffle pattern is the 6th of the scale. And that's all you really need for that classic shuffle riff. If it were in the key of E, then E would be the root, B would be the 5th, and C♯ would be the 6th.

So the E shuffle riff would look like this:

A common variation adds the ♭7th as well, which would be a D note.

 (0:20)

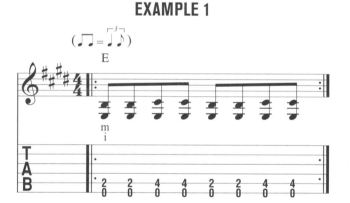

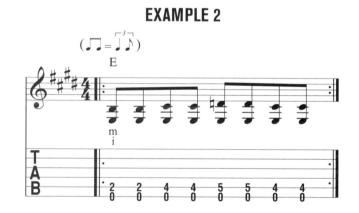

And again, this same riff can be transposed to A or D just by playing on different string sets.

EXAMPLE 3

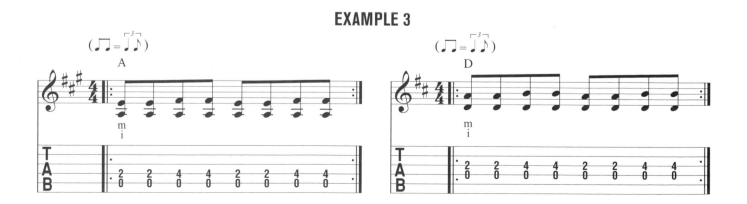

Also important is the rhythmic composition of what the shuffle lick entails. Although it's typical to count the riff as "one-and, two-and, three-and, four-and," there's actually an implied triplet feel going on. In other words, each beat is divided into three equal parts instead of two. What this means is, when you see eighth notes written along with the shuffled (or "swung") eighth notes indication: ($\sqcap$ = $\overset{3}{\overline{}}$), the first note is basically twice as long as the second. This creates the lopsided, shuffling kind of sound and rhythm. Of course, this riff can be played as "straight" (normal) eighth notes too, à la Chuck Berry (think "Johnny B. Goode") and many others, and the notes are all the same. But the shuffle feel is much more common in the blues.

Now, when we talk about harmony shuffles, we are looking at the shuffle licks in a harmonized manner. We do this by adding notes on the third string that will move in harmony with the notes on the fifth string. This new set of notes will start on the major 3rd of the chord (G♯ in the key of E) and will move one fret up to the 4th (A) of the scale and then two more frets to the 5th (B). This movement harmonizes with the other moving string (fifth string), which moves to the 5th (B), 6th (C♯), and ♭7th (D).

Here's what the basic pattern will look like for the E chord.

 (2:15)

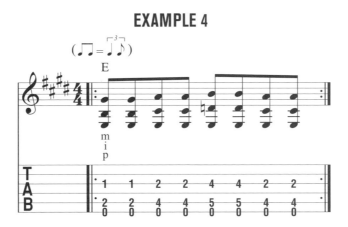

As you can see from the video, this can be accomplished by "grabbing" three strings, one with the thumb and the other two with two fingers. An alternate fingerpicking approach can involve changing the riff so the thumb plays both the lowest note of the shuffle and then the note right after it. This means you can essentially reduce the lick to only two fingers, rather than three, which would look like this:

 (3:08)

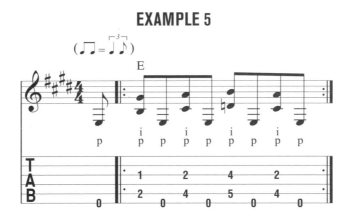

I still prefer the three-fingered approach, but it's good to know both ways of playing it. Another common variation sort of combines both approaches. We're using the thumb to play constant eighth notes, but we're only sounding the harmony notes on the beats, like this:

 (5:35)

EXAMPLE 6

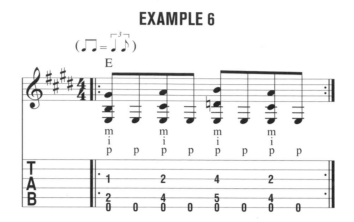

And for yet another variation, we can add the open high E string for a triplet pattern.

 (8:07)

EXAMPLE 7

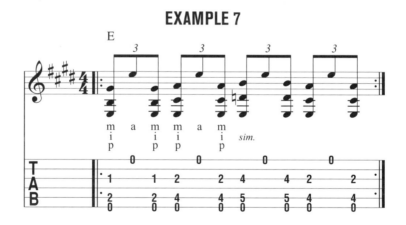

A Chord Harmony Shuffle

It's a little trickier when moving to A, but it's still doable. We'll use a barred A chord with our pinky up on the high A note at fret 5 of the high E string. It looks like this:

 (8:40)

EXAMPLE 8

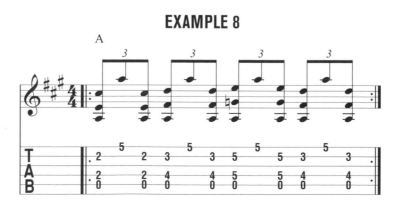

And again, there are numerous variations you can employ with this pattern. You can hear me play the following A-chord variation earlier in the video during a 12-bar jam in E.

 (1:09)

EXAMPLE 9

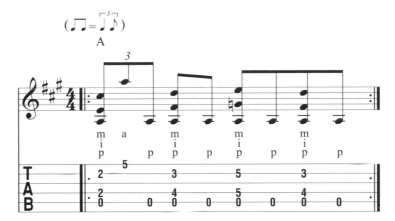

D Chord Harmony Shuffle

The D form of the harmony shuffle is different still from the E and A forms. I most commonly play it in eighth notes like this:

 (10:54)

EXAMPLE 10

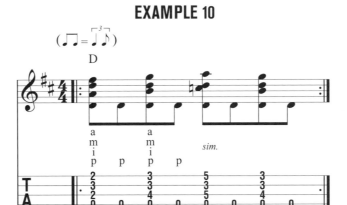

A triplet-based variation on that might look like this:

EXAMPLE 11

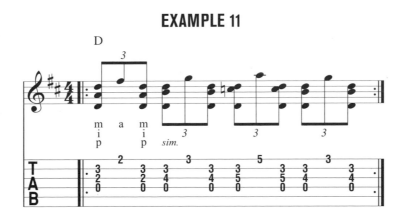

Turnarounds

As I continue on this fingerstyle journey, we can see it also applies to turnaround licks. I demonstrate the basic one for E in both high-E string and low-E string versions. The low E version is cool, because it involves what we refer to as a *10th voicing*, which means it has a *split octave* (the distance of an octave plus a 3rd). It's also interesting because this utilizes the string played by the thumb in this case. Musically it is changed; physically it really isn't.

Here's a basic turnaround in E:

 (5:50)

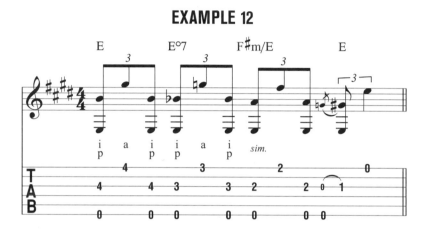

Now here's the version where the notes on the high E string are moved down to the low E string. And our high E becomes the drone. That looks like this:

 (7:09)

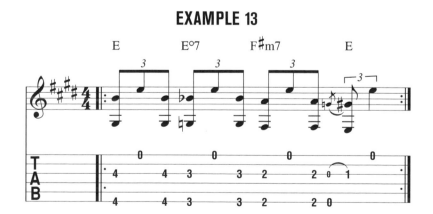

A Word About Turnarounds

Remember that a turnaround is called such since it involves the last two measures of a 12-bar blues, essentially "turning" the progression around to start again at the beginning. The problem comes from the excessive use of turnaround licks, which can be far too repetitive, boring, and overly used, even by some of the best guitarists around. To this I say, learn the turnaround licks, use them, and then forget them! By this I mean, use these licks as a basis for many other musical moments besides the turnaround itself, and you'll see they are really no more than riffs that can be used in a million musical ways–not just the purely predictable ones. This is an important thing to always keep in mind. I much prefer to create an original-sounding blues lick in place of a traditional turnaround lick!

The Open E Blues Box Scale

In the video demonstration, where I play the open E blues box position, you can see how I am using the thumb as a dampening or muting tool. The thumb plays a critical role here in allowing only certain strings to ring out while keeping the others quiet. This, again, is a concept many guitarists have a hard time grasping, since it involves the "silent" work of the fingers, as well as the "audible" work. As I will continue to drive home, the fingers almost always have two jobs to perform: sounding a note (or notes) and stopping a note (or notes)! What you don't hear is just as crucial as what you do hear, and the process of doing this must become second nature to the real player!

So, as you can see, in this open E box scale, I am working all the way down to the low E string by plucking with the fingers. The thumb is lying across whatever strings are not needed at the time and slowly allowing each new string to be sounded as it becomes part of the run.

 (4:27)

EXAMPLE 14

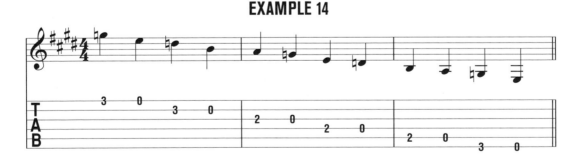

CHAPTER 3:
ALTERNATING BASS, TRAVIS PICKING, AND RAGTIME GUITAR

In this section, I discuss the alternating bass and the wonderful format of ragtime guitar. The art of incorporating the bass parts, usually the alternating variety, really gives this style its personality. The thumb is far more active in this technique than with the constant bass, and for some, it may even seem easier, even though it's far more complex.

Travis Picking

The beauty of Merle Travis' style was that he could really play an entire song, and all of its aspects, with just his own two hands. Most folks think it was just an alternating bass underneath a higher melody, but in actuality, the thumb usually alternated between a bass note and then a strummed chord fragment. The melody "on top" was only played by Merle's index finger, so if he needed to create a more complex melody or lick, he would have to incorporate the thumb as well as the index finger.

The alternating bass is usually created when you are in an open chord position such as E, A, or D, but the C and G positions are equally fruitful for melodic and rhythmic possibilities. Most of these kinds of bass patterns involve alternating octaves of the same note, but often they also use the root and 5th, or even the root, 3rd, and 5th. Obviously, when you do this, you are making the pattern far more complex, and the intertwining of melody and rhythm are far more intricate.

Heel Dampening

The art of *heel dampening* with the picking hand is another real specialty of fingerstyle that Merle Travis utilized and perfected, and it serves to further define the bass part as sounding a lot more like an upright bass. This is because it creates shorter note decays, just like an upright, and it tends to muffle the tone of those notes, eliminating most of their highs.

The effect is created similarly to the *palm mute* technique in rock guitar. You simply touch the strings with the edge of your palm right in front of the bridge. The farther in from the bridge you are, the more muted the sound becomes. By using this technique, you'll notice that the higher, lead part can now dance over the top of the bass more than before, and the two parts are now much more distinct and tonally separated.

 (1:20)

EXAMPLE 1

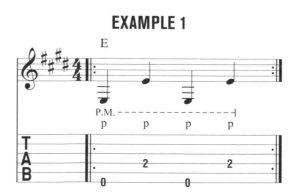

EXAMPLE 2

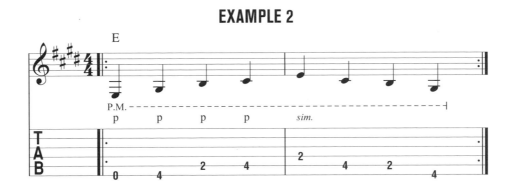

Of course, you don't have to dampen the bass if you don't want. That's the great thing about fingerstyle guitar; you have so many choices. Here's a nice little Travis picking riff that I demonstrate both ways on the video—with dampening and without—so you can hear the difference.

▶ (1:44)

EXAMPLE 3

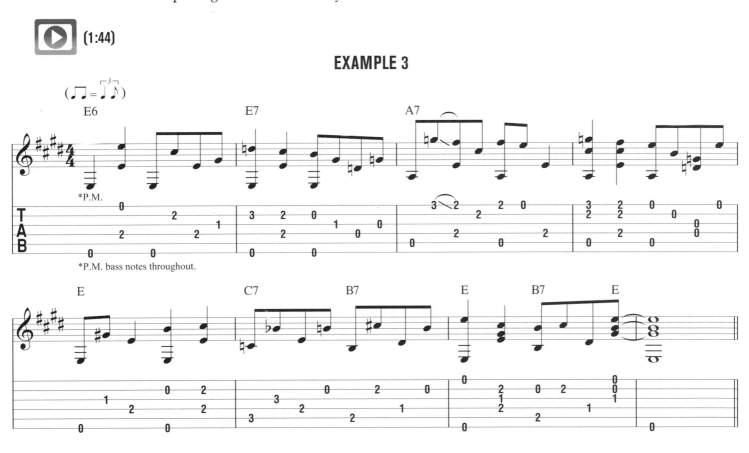

Some players like to call the typical folk fingerpicking style Travis picking, which looks something like this:

▶ (2:37)

EXAMPLE 4

But that's not *really* Travis picking, because it lacks the "bounce" and the muted bass. The Travis-picked version would sound more like this:

 (2:47)

A Note on the Alternating Bass

As I had mentioned previously, the alternating bass is essential to the true Travis style, and the proper bounce that can be achieved with this technique is best when you use accent strokes with the thumb of the picking hand. This means that you land on the next string after each bass note is played. So, in other words, when you play the low E string, you then stop the thumb's motion by landing on the A string. This controls how far the thumb has to travel each time you strike the string. Also, and just as importantly, it serves to mute that A string. The next E note that is played by the thumb is one octave higher on the D string, and once again we land on the next string, which this time is the G string. So in essence, we have gained complete control over the bottom four strings of the guitar, leaving very little chance for error while keeping the notes clean and the rhythm crisp.

You'll also note that this accent stroke enables you to intensify your attack and volume if needed, while keeping the thumb from "getting away from you." Once again, the distance and attack is controlled, and we needn't interfere with any of the higher, melodic notes in the piece.

There are times, as you'll see me discuss in the video portion, when I need to leave the alternating bass so I can reach higher notes up the fretboard. I will then move to a straight, constant bass that still gives the listener the sense of bass being played. We're not alternating octaves, but it still has the same effect of "filling it out" and keeping a sense of time happening. It may take a while to master this particular technique, but you'll soon discover that it's a great survival technique for anyone aspiring to solo fingerstyle mastery!

The Ragtime Style

The fingerpicked ragtime approach was really popularized in the 1920s by artists such as Blind Blake, Scrapper Blackwell, Blind Willie McTell, Leadbelly, and several more, all of whom loved to emulate the piano of that era. I'm sure that it was not uncommon for one musician playing in this way to be able to keep an entire room of people dancing thanks to the bouncing style.

Ragtime is easily one of the more truly satisfying styles on the guitar, since it utilizes the entire range of the instrument, particularly in the open positions. The key of C is perhaps the most perfectly adapted open position for this style, as it can have an alternating bass that uses three strings—notably the E, A, and D strings. Sometimes, as you'll see, when I alternate to the low G note on the low E string, I may actually quickly play a G or G7 chord to go with it, further emphasizing the stride piano simulation that works so well.

"Diddie Wah Diddie"

There is hardly a better song in the guitar kingdom that can illustrate the great ragtime style better than "Diddie Wah Diddie," a mildly risqué song by none other than the inimitable Blind Blake. A true master of his craft, Blake has influenced generations of players such as Ry Cooder, Leon Redbone, and myself, and I also believe that there is a not-so-distant connection between this style of the '20s and the Travis styles of the '40s and '50s also!

Here's the "A" section of the tune.

EXAMPLE 6

*T = Thumb on 6th string.

**Flick i finger down to strum strings.

As you'll see in my demonstration of this piece on the video, there are several moves that make this song an intriguing blend of technique, artistry, and humor, which certainly points to its vaudevillian origins. Its entertainment factor was just as important as anything else.

The instrumental break, which utilizes walking octaves, dissonance, and other cool techniques, is definitely meant to entertain not only the audience, but quite obviously the player too! As I have always said with ragtime guitar, "thank God for open C," because it just so perfectly lends itself to a nice, solid format in which to create patterns. You also have the ability to work a bit outside the open C area while not totally losing the momentum of playing in the open position and keeping the rhythm going!

Fretting with the thumb is a technique that is looked down upon by classical players and teachers, but it certainly works well within ragtime, blues, and folk techniques, for sure. Perhaps the most necessary place for this to be used is with an F chord. This enables us to avoid having to play a big, fat barre chord just to accommodate this position. Rather, it gives us a nice, warm-sounding low F note that we can still play our standard F chord over. Again, you'll see this demonstrated in the video. It does tend to lock up the fretting hand a bit, since we are actually gripping the whole neck where the frets are the widest, so you can see that in my playing the instrumental, I am really only afforded one bending opportunity on the B string—with the pinky, no less! It's still very effective, though! And as I keep emphasizing, any note usually also involves the creation of a "silent" note, and in this case, the thumb also serves to eliminate that A string by just touching it as we fret the low E string with it. Also, as I illustrate in the video, you see how it is a highly movable position that lends itself to being shifted up and down the entire neck. It is simply a great alternative to the traditional E-form barre chord that, in many cases, is quite a bit more flexible than we are used to with the traditional approach.

As I also illustrate in the video, we can see that the fretting hand has a very important role in its ability to "squeeze" notes and chords when needed. I go a little off topic here, where I illustrate what would be straight strum techniques to show how the fretting hand can lift off certain chords and notes, enabling the strumming hand to not lose sight of the rhythm pattern being created. This is the kind of thing that really can't be written in music, as it utilizes "ghost notes" that become part of the percussive effect of what we are doing. This is accomplished by the fretting hand not actually lifting off the strings, but by simply not pressing the chords or notes down to the fretboard. In this manner, we create those nice, little clicks and whacks that give us the ability to use the fretting hand as the pulse and "drummer" behind the drive of the piece.

Getting back to the "Diddie Wah Diddie" piece, we can see how nice it is to be able to play that alternating bass over the F chord, while also gripping the neck, enabling us to play that little bend on the B string. This alone is a good technique and style to focus on, and you'll see that you can find many other uses for this kind of riff in other situations.

Here's the "B" section of the song:

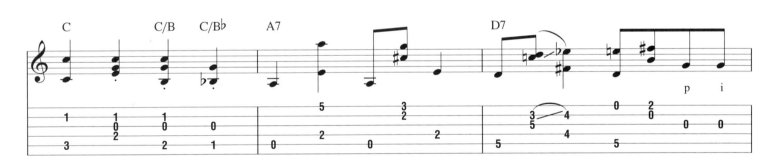
(8:47)

EXAMPLE 7

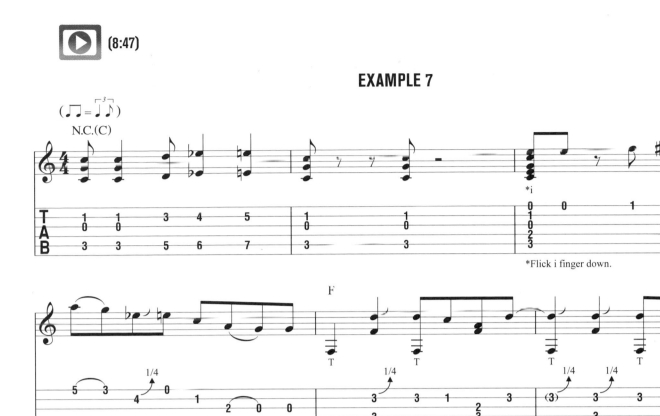

*Flick i finger down.

CHAPTER 4:
"I AM A PILGRIM" AND ROCKABILLY STYLE

I Am a Pilgrim

During some of Merle Travis' earlier work, he pretty much stayed with an acoustic guitar and played a lot of very personal songs in a nice, relaxed solo performer manner. "I Am a Pilgrim" was one where he truly combined a gospel/bluesy feeling with a rural-sounding song to evoke a very personal and emotional result. It was very supportive of his vocals, which is what you want, but, because of its melodic content, was also locked in with the melody he was singing. Because it's down in the open E position as well as the higher, middle-of-the-neck A position, we are leaning more towards a kind of blues style that uses 7ths, major 3rd hammer-ons, and other bluesy techniques, while still making use of a nice, alternating bass pattern.

Here's a basic accompaniment version:

▶ (0:34)

EXAMPLE 1

The key to really seeing if this pattern is working is to compare the accompanying part behind the vocal to the way we approach the actual solo, which then takes over the melody for itself. Many of the pickup notes and phrases that were at first played along with the vocal are now played on their own during the solo, and played more emphatically as the melody.

Also of note is how the closed position of A, in fifth position, still lends itself to certain nice, open-string usage. This, once again, shows you just how multi-faceted and versatile fingerpicking can be!

Here's a solo-style version I play at the beginning of this video chapter.

 (0:01)

EXAMPLE 2

Rockabilly Style

Rockabilly players, such as Carl Perkins and Scotty Moore, would adapt this style and use it as a backdrop for those uptempo numbers as well. This often made use of closed positions. Here's an Example of a Perkins-style riff in A. Notice that, although we're in fifth position here, we're still using the open A string as our lowest bass note. Also note how you can simply move the same chord form down a set of strings and get a nice augmented V chord. In this case, it becomes E+.

▶ (4:44)

EXAMPLE 3

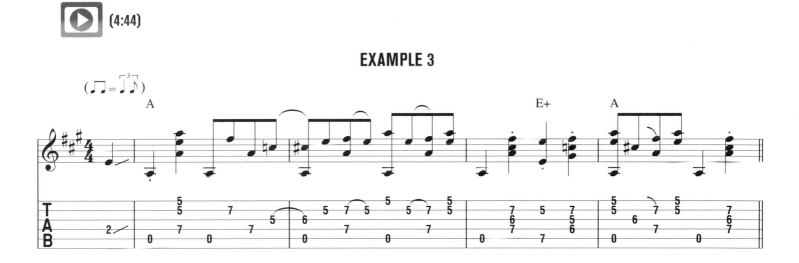

Of course, you can really apply this to any key—even something as non-guitar-friendly as B♭. It really helps to use the left-hand thumb to handle the bass notes in this case, as it frees up the pinky for adding melody notes.

▶ (6:40)

EXAMPLE 4

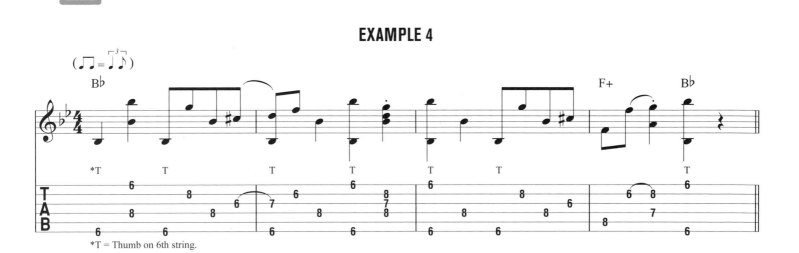

*T = Thumb on 6th string.

CHAPTER 5:
MORE HARMONY SHUFFLES

We can expand the harmony shuffles we learned earlier by using *triple stops*, or three-note groups. This requires an accurate plucking approach that uses the thumb for the bass and three fingers in a row for the triple stops on top. It may be a bit tricky at first, but with a little practice, you won't have to look at your right-hand fingers at all, as they should always be "at the ready" to play those notes and/or stop them from ringing after plucking them. If you utilize the accent stroke with the thumb, you will always be landing on the next string, thereby keeping perfect time, muting the string you land on, and not interfering with any of the higher strings. That's a lot of stuff to make happen with one little accent stroke, but it's very true!

Here's the basic pattern in E:

 (2:44)

EXAMPLE 1

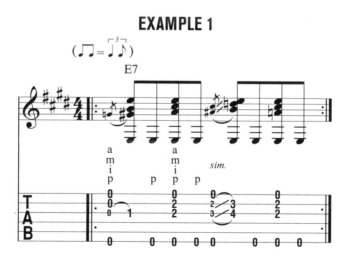

Just be sure to always keep that thumb out in front, so there is no collision happening between the index finger and the thumb.

For the IV chord, A7, you can make a slight adjustment to the first triple stop, lowering G♯ to G, and play the same thing.

 (3:06)

EXAMPLE 2

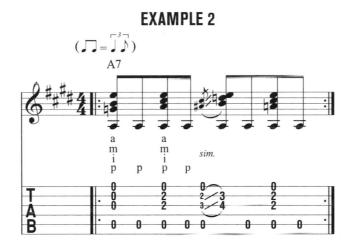

For the V chord in measure 9 of a 12-bar blues in E, you would most likely just play a pattern using the open B7 chord. The following A7 in measure 10 is a great place to insert a lick before the turnaround. So you could play something like this, starting from measure 9:

 (3:19)

EXAMPLE 3

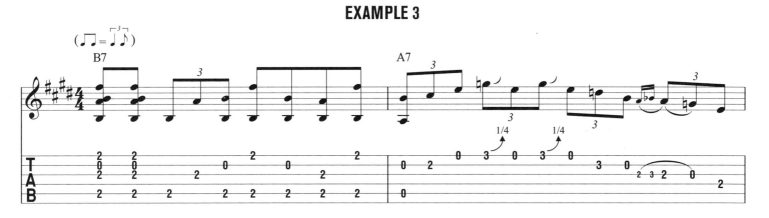

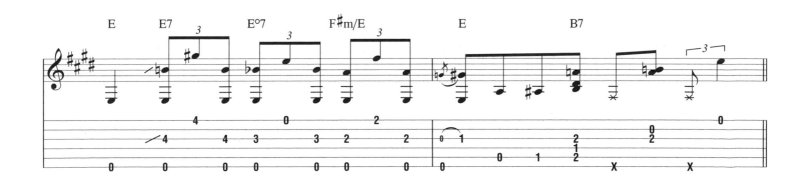

"Cruisin' Coupe"

I used a variation of this idea for my song, "Cruisin' Coupe," which appeared on my *Drive It Home* album and was dedicated to my dear friend, the late, great Danny Gatton. This song is played at a faster tempo and with a straight-eighths feel, but you'll recognize the same elements as in the triple-stop harmony shuffle we just looked at.

 (5:16)

EXAMPLE 4

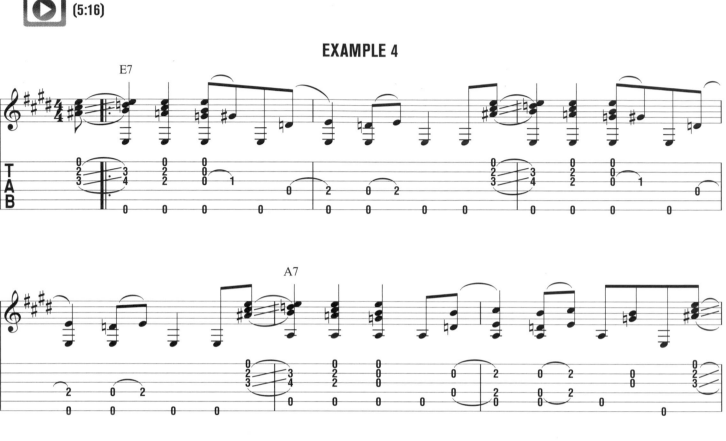

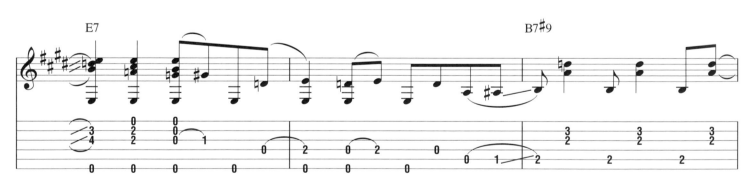

Train Whistle

There's a great scene in the movie *Crossroads* where Joe Seneca tells Ralph Macchio to play the sound of a train on his guitar after he demonstrates on his harmonica. Here's an example that's similar to what I played for that scene. For the double stop—the "whistle"— be sure that you're only bending string 2 (not string 1) and only slightly. It's not quite a half step; it's "in the cracks." This is answered by another variation of the harmony shuffle riff, played in straight eighths, in which I'm using a lot of fret-hand muting. Only the notes on strings 6, 5, and 3 should sound, alternated with fully muted dead strums on the upbeats. I'm plucking this riff with my fingers, but I'm just using the nail of my index finger and thumb like a pick.

 (8:56)

EXAMPLE 5

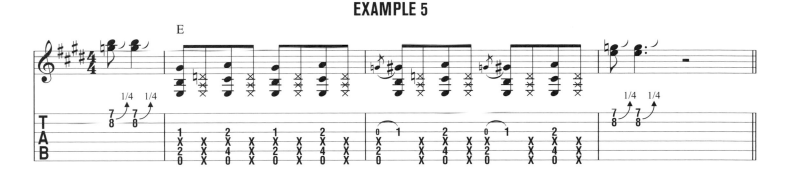

And here's a nice little lick I like to do with the whistle bend. While I'm holding that bend, I pull off to the open high E string from the seventh and ninth frets and then pluck the pre-bent G note on string 2 for a triplet rhythm.

 (10:31)

EXAMPLE 6

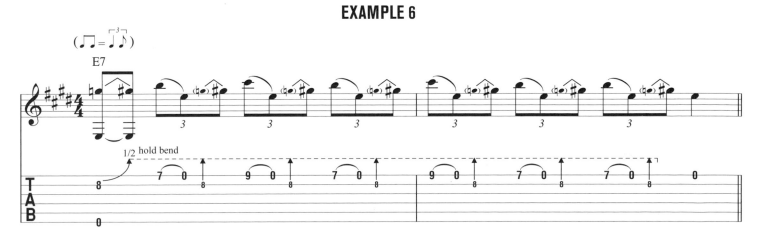

You can also make this lick work over A7 by releasing the bend to a G note and playing the same thing over an A bass note, like this:

 (10:37)

EXAMPLE 7

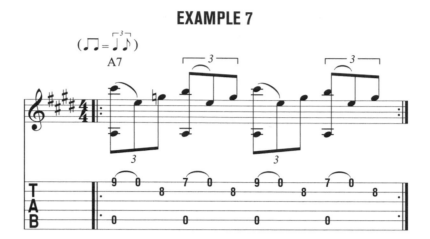

Let's close out here with a full example demonstrating how we can incorporate the whistle bend into a shuffle piece. This one also has a fancy turnaround that you may have not heard before.

 (11:45)

EXAMPLE 8

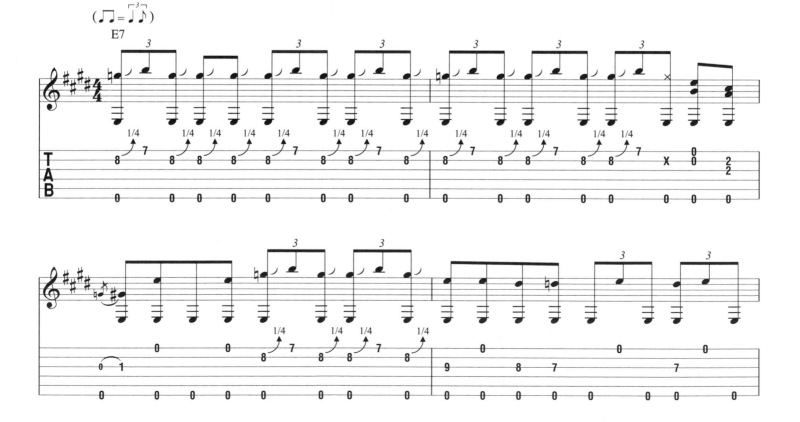

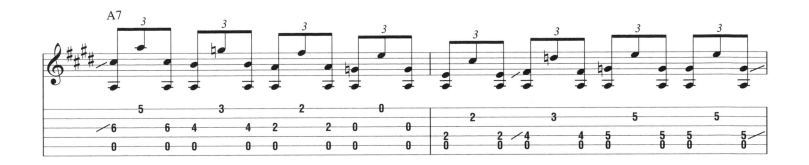

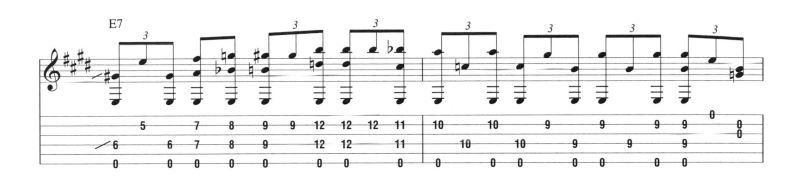

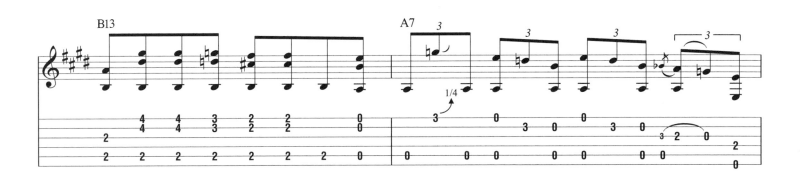

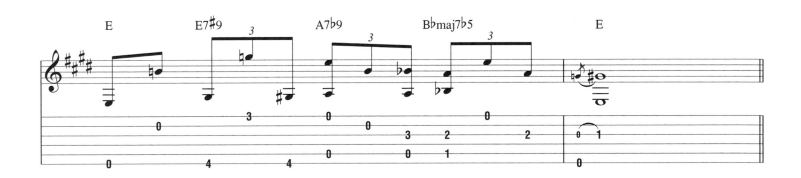

CHAPTER 6:
THE "MYSTERY TRAIN" LICK

This is the final installment in this book and a very important one at that! In the case of this kind of right-hand pattern, we find it very important to utilize the alternating bass, especially in the open E position.

With regards to my muting theory, this pattern demonstrates it beautifully. Again, I'll stress that when we play the low E string and then the middle E on the D string, we are not jumping over the A string to get there. This is a common misconception among fingerpickers, and I see it quite often with my students. It's far better to use the thumb to create accent strokes as it plays the E and then the D strings. In this manner, the thumb lands on the A, thereby muting it, and then it's ready to play the D string. If you really examine this technique, it's a beautiful and very compact way of dealing with the bottom strings. It keeps them well under control and keeps the bass notes clear of the higher "lead" strings.

Also, by using the accent strokes, we are keeping the power and drive of those alternating E bass notes contained, and we can ease up on them or really lean into them, depending on the volume we want. In either case, the strings will still be contained, as will our thumb, and the higher strings will be free to use in any matter we choose.

Having said that, let's take a look at the basic "Mystery Train" pattern, which was used to drive many songs of the early rock 'n' roll era.

 (1:00)

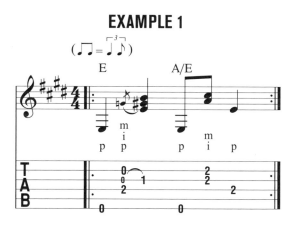

As a variation, sometimes I'll add the open high E string on top, like this:

 (1:51)

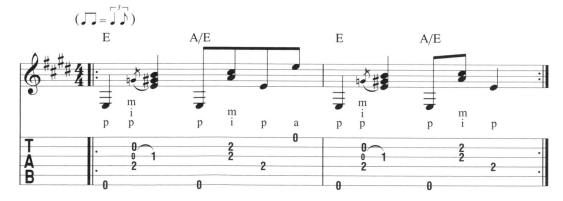

A common tendency among beginners is to use the index finger for that second bass note on the D string; they're usually not even aware that they've unconsciously changed the thumb pattern to a "thumb and finger" bass pattern. It may sound right, but in actuality, it's a shortcut. It may produce the right notes, but it totally disrupts that nice, driving bass note pattern! So, always stay aware of this possible mistake, and be sure to keep those bass notes driving ahead!

Over the IV chord, A7, you often see this type of pattern, with a little melody on top.

(2:40)

EXAMPLE 3

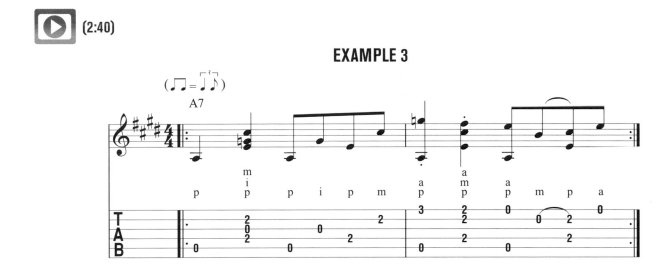

Over the V chord in measure 9, I play a standard alternating bass pattern on the open B7, much like the ones we've seen before in previous chapters. In measure 10, however, I like to play a banjo-style fill in which I'll bring my thumb up to string 3 and use my *i* and *m* fingers on strings 2 and 1, respectively. It looks like this:

(3:00)

EXAMPLE 4

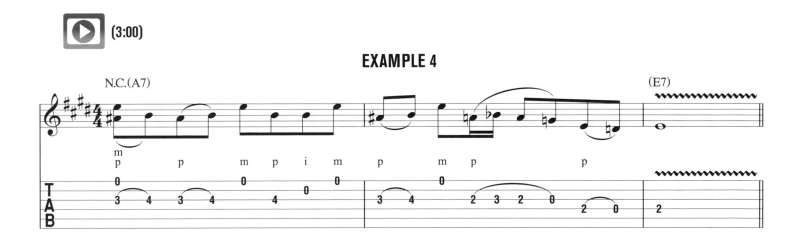

It's also common to pluck the open B string along with the hammer-ons from the third to fourth fret, as I demonstrate on the video.

CONCLUSION

In summation, I can say it has truly been a pleasure, and I hope that all my extensive experience in this technique and style has helped you move ahead. I know that, over the years, my need to keep on teaching these styles has led to more and more understanding of what to look for and what to avoid. Most of all, I have always found that my best learning curve has been through teaching and learning just what makes *me* tick.

Remember that I'm nothing but a largely self-taught musician who likes to pass it on to others who, in the end, also love to continue their self-learning process! Fingerstyle is perhaps the most overall satisfying way to play the guitar, and I hope I have helped further the process for you!

—Arlen Roth, 2017